A Love Story from

TRINIDAD

2007-8 NMI
MISSION EDUCATION RESOURCES

✳ ✳ ✳

BOOKS

AFRICA'S SOUL HOPE
The AIDS Crisis and the Church
by Ellen Decker

BABOONS ON THE RUNWAY
And Other Humorous Stories from Africa
by Richard F. Zanner

MEETING JESUS
by Keith Schwanz

THE NUDGE IN MY SIDE
Stories from Indonesia and the Philippines
by The Bob McCroskeys

THEY SAW ONLY FEET
More Life Lessons from Missionary Kids
by Dean Nelson

A LOVE STORY FROM TRINIDAD
by Ruth O. Saxon

✳ ✳ ✳

ADULT MISSION EDUCATION RESOURCE BOOK

RESPONDING TO MISSION CHALLENGES
Editors: Aimee Curtis and Rosanne Bolerjack

A Love Story from

TRINIDAD

Ruth O. Saxon

Nazarene Publishing House
Kansas City, Missouri

Copyright 2007
Nazarene Publishing House

ISBN-13: 978-0-8341-2292-5
ISBN-10: 0-8341-2292-8

Printed in the United States of America

Editor: Aimee Curtis
Cover Design: Keith Alexander
Interior Design: Sharon Page

10 9 8 7 6 5 4 3 2 1

DEDICATION

To the glory of God, whose love made the story possible, and to all the CNTC students who loved and labored with me in Chanka Trace

CONTENTS

Ruth O. Saxon

was a missionary for the Church of the Nazarene, serving 43 years in Trinidad. Her assignment for the entire time was at Caribbean Nazarene Theological College (now Caribbean Nazarene College), where she held various positions—professor, academic dean, and interim president.

Ruth earned a bachelor's degree at George Peabody College (now Peabody College of Vanderbilt University) in Tennessee. She also earned the master of divinity and doctor of ministry degrees from Nazarene Theological Seminary. She was ordained by Dr. Hardy C. Powers in Mississippi just prior to leaving for the mission field.

Ruth was the 6th of 12 children born to Rev. John and Sara Saxon. Cradled in the Church of the Nazarene, she grew up realizing the importance and value of both a Christian family and the church.

During her final furlough in 1996-97, she taught and served as missionary-in-residence at Mount Vernon Nazarene College (now Mount Vernon Nazarene University). Since then she has joyfully served as a volunteer teacher at Asia-Pacific Nazarene Theological Seminary and in the extension program for Caribbean Nazarene College in Belize, Bahamas, and Guyana, the latter four times. She makes her home at the Bradenton Missionary Retirement Village in Florida.

Dr. Saxon is the author of the 1970-71 NMI reading book *Flares in the Night*, republished in 1990-91, and *Triumph in Trinidad* published in 2002-3.

INTRODUCTION

How do you fall in love with a village? A village with a bad reputation? A village known as Coke City? A village passed off by some on the opposite side of the highway as full of criminals?

I can only describe how it happened to me.

Very soon after the Lord tapped me to work for Him in Chanka Trace—a small village in El Socorro, Trinidad—I realized I could be in trouble if people didn't know me and why I was there. I set about to make friends and open myself to being known. Previous experience of church people seemed to incline residents to trust both me and students from Caribbean Nazarene Theological College (CNTC). We freely introduced ourselves. We visited from house to house and chatted on the streets.

People responded in love. They invited us to their Hindu weddings. I wept genuine tears with the bereaved at funerals and sometimes, by request, spoke briefly. On DiVali night (the Hindu festival of lights), after the religious ceremonies were over, I visited homes and enjoyed the fellowship and food.

When I had overseas visitors (relatives, friends, and Work and Witness volunteers), I introduced them to the boys on the block waiting for drug customers. It was a way of recognizing even drug pushers as human beings loved by God. In time, I felt assured they knew I disapproved of their occupation but truly loved them.

Eventually I felt like an honored citizen. I was told, "Your car is safe here, night or day, locked or unlocked." I think, if necessary, villagers would have fought for my personal protection. I never lived in Chanka Trace, but I was only a phone call away and visited much more than at church time. Duty sometimes called me there late at night, but I knew both God and my friends were watching. I felt safer than anywhere else in Trinidad, except in my own home. Students were also assured that they were safe.

I became known at the area police station as an advocate for villagers who were in trouble. One day I went to the desk sergeant, a new one to me, and told him who I was before stating my business. "Oh," he interrupted, "you're the lady from the church." I made several visits on behalf of others to a Christian lawyer friend. The second time I came to her with a possible case of murder, she asked tongue-in-cheek, "Did you do something bad in a previous life that you're always in the middle of such trouble?"

Was I ever taken advantage of? You'd better believe it. Such as the time a mother pled for money to take a son sick with chicken pox to the doctor. He had chicken pox all right—months before. I hope she used well what I gave her. Or the time when an

Moya and her son Michael

addict said he was hungry and needed bread. I took him to a store, bought bread and several things to go with it. He ate the bread, sold the rest, and doubtless got another fix. I've worked long and lovingly with addicts who seemed to want rehabilitation, only to have them go back to drugs. Disappointing love does not kill it, however.

All of the above did not cause me to fall in love with Chanka Trace, though. The flame was lit much earlier.

Only weeks after we began services in this area of Trinidad, a lady named Moya came forward and gave her heart to Jesus. The next night she was back and testified of the amazing joy she had.

"I've worked hard all day, and I'm not the least bit tired," she exclaimed.

Spontaneously my heart overflowed with love, not just for Moya but for the whole community. Standing to my feet, I declared, "Chanka Trace, I love you!"

I am convinced what I feel is more than natural human love. It is God loving Chanka Trace, and He is pleased to do it through me. What a gracious privilege!

Ruth O. Saxon

One
IN THE BEGINNING

The small Indian teenager stood a few feet in front of me. Alone, in the midst of other seekers. Crying, convicted of his sins during the anointed preaching.

A pastor on the platform caught my eye and motioned me alongside.

"Son, may I help you pray?" I offered.

"Please do," he sobbed.

After a little instruction, together we prayed, "Lord Jesus, I know that I am a sinner. I confess my sins to You and ask You to forgive them all. Come into my heart to live. I give myself to You."

He was so sincere that very quickly this seeker had become a glad finder. The Christ who convicted his heart had indeed forgiven him and come to live within.

"May I have your name please?"

"Robby Mungroo," was his reply

I wrote it down. I knew only one other family by that name—my "adopted" daughter and her folks.

"Are you related to Esther Mungroo?" I asked gently.

"Cousins. She knows exactly where I live."

Robby Mungroo

I turned the name in to one of the leaders of the crusade, a united effort by all the local Nazarene churches on the island. It was held mid-September 1984 on the Queen's Park Savannah in Port of Spain, Trinidad.

A few weeks later I visited Santa Cruz Old Road Church of the Nazarene during their local crusade. To my delight, Esther had come with her husband, along with Robby and his sister Savi. We chatted awhile after the service.

"Would you please visit our mother?" Savi asked. "She's giving us a hard time." Esther filled me in on the details. The Hindu parents were distressed that their children had become Christians. At first I pled that I was busy, but hearing that Robby had threatened suicide, I knew I must try to help.

Late the next afternoon, when all I absolutely had to do was completed, I decided to pay that visit. I drove to Esther's home so she could go with me, but she was away. Her mother-in-law was sure I could find the Mungroo family just by asking.

The wanderings of the day before were far from wasted. I had seen what God wanted me to see— a whole community with only one visible sign of a Christian church.

"You drive across the highway and ask anybody for Doggie Mungroo. That's Robby's father. Everybody knows him."

I tried it. I had been in that community maybe only one other time in my life, with someone who knew where she was going. Now I drove up one street and down another, asking anyone I saw for directions. No one seemed to know Robby or his father. Just after sundown, I was invited into the home of a very friendly Muslim lady. We chatted enough to know that we liked each other. But she didn't know Doggie Mungroo either. As I started to leave, she advised: "Don't stay here late, but you come back." I promised I would (a promise I kept many times).

The next afternoon, determined to try again, I neared the exit gate to leave the CNTC campus when Esther came walking in. Her mother-in-law had told her of my quest the day before, and now she had come to accompany me. With her guidance we drove straight to the home in a small community off to one side of Chanka Trace. The visit was well received, and the Mungroos and I became good friends.

But the wanderings of the day before were far from wasted. I had seen what God wanted me to see—a whole community with only one visible sign of a Christian church. And it was a small structure crammed between a house on the front and a factory on the back. (In time I came to understand it was a group whose people mostly came from outside, congregating there for worship on Sunday. There seemed to be little effort to reach out to the locals.)

God wouldn't let me forget what I had seen. He didn't tell me this part of El Socorro was considered dangerous—so dangerous that some people on the other side of the highway were afraid to drive their cars there even in the daytime. He didn't tell me it was known as "Coke City" and that it lived up to its name. In time I understood this and much more.

When a previous El Socorro Church of the Nazarene existed, it was located on the northern ("good") side of the highway. It had been sponsored by Santa Cruz Old Road Church of the Nazarene during my

Esther

pastorate, then a student from CNTC took over—the first of many. But when the owner asked us to vacate the rented quarters, the pastor was simply assigned elsewhere, and the furnishings we had so lovingly gathered were given out to other local churches. That left 10 charter members, including Esther, adrift. How could anything good come out of that?

God, in His wisdom, found a way. Esther and her husband, needing a church nearby, had gathered with members of a church with a different worship style and theology. Because of the differences, they never joined but willingly crossed the highway to Chanka Trace to hold an afternoon Sunday School.

For Esther, it was more like reconnecting with her roots. She had lived part of her childhood "over the highway," as it was called. This was also an occasion to get closer to the Mungroos who lived on that side, as well as become reacquainted with old friends and make new ones. But she and her husband still kept ties to Santa Cruz Old Road Church of the Nazarene, attending when they could afford gas money for their old car. And it was to that big crusade in the Savannah that she had proudly brought Robby and his sister.

In the meantime, I was beginning to feel less and less at home in the local church I had been attending. My presence seemed to put the pastor in a bind. Wednesday night services were given over to a parachurch ministry for Christian education. I avoided coming for a while, but figuring the course must be over, I ventured down a little late one Wednesday night. All was quiet inside, but a stranger met me at the door.

"Come right in," he cheerfully encouraged. "We're just taking an examination."

Already a professor at CNTC, I didn't want to find myself in yet another classroom. So I thanked him and returned home.

"Lord," I prayed, "I need some place to go to church."

And so the Divine Mathematician put several pieces together to make a beautiful whole. I needed somewhere to work and worship. Chanka Trace needed a church. And Esther was already an insider. The group she worked with sometimes held crusades in Chanka Trace, but at the conclusion they invited interested persons to come to their church on the opposite side of the highway. It seems few ever came, and perhaps only one real convert resulted from their efforts. Undoubtedly Chanka Trace needed a church of its own.

We began with a Wednesday night service on January 16, 1985, in Esther's apartment. Specifically we prayed for God to give us an entrance into Chanka Trace. Other interested persons soon joined us, including Aziz and Bella Abidh—students at CNTC. Bella had relatives living over the highway. Then there were Wayne and Marva Woods, members of St. James Church of the Nazarene, but living within a mile or two of Chanka Trace. Shirley and Esau Alladin, members of the Felicity Church of the Nazarene, rented an apartment within walking distance, and they also joined us. We began collecting an offering each Wednesday, holding the money for the purpose of start-up expenses. Our target date for the initial crusade was April 7—Easter Sunday.

Wayne Woods was an excellent furniture maker. He fashioned a nice pulpit, still in use today. In two Saturdays we built four backless benches and made a sturdy platform out of heavy plywood. Then we arranged everything, including 100 rented chairs, in a large open shed on Temple Street. We were excited. The next day was Easter when we planned to have our first crusade service. We distributed handbills, installed lightbulbs, and lifted fervent prayers heavenward.

Unbeknown to us, a Hindu wedding was to take place on Temple Street that Easter Sunday. Just as we arrived to begin readying things for the evening service, traffic erupted out of the one-lane street, cars driving backward in great haste, people running for safety. It seems that the local bride (or was it the groom?) was marrying someone from a rival community, and a fight had broken out between the two factions. Sensing there was no possibility of a service that night, we quickly left for home. Our first service would have to be Monday night.

Two
EARLY CRATEWOOD CHAPEL

"Good evening, friends! We welcome you to our crusade, sponsored by the Church of the Nazarene."

With these words we began on Monday night, April 8, 1985, with 30 people in attendance—a good start considering that Easter Monday is a holiday. We figured others listened and looked from a safe distance out in the dark. Our core group of Nazarenes was there, as well as a new Christian friend, Goura Mohammed, who lived just two doors away. She was the one visible fruit of the crusades held previously by the church Esther used to attend.

The services continued for a full two weeks. Attendance fluctuated, hitting a low of 15 due to another Hindu wedding, and a high of 89. Usually it was between 60 and 70 per night. During the second week, we conducted a children's crusade in the afternoons with attendance reaching as high as 70 in several services.

"We do not intend to leave after the crusade. We plan to stay and start a church right here," we announced boldly in our public services. We had permission from the owner of the shed to continue using it. And so the last Sunday of the crusade, April 21, was the first Sunday of regular services, complete with an 11:00 morning worship service, an afternoon Sunday School, and the closing crusade service in the evening.

One Sunday morning we arrived for service only to find ducks swimming on the floor of our shed.

I did most of the preaching at first, assisted by Aziz Abidh, while Wayne Woods made an able song director. Then on Father's Day, June 16, it was a privilege to announce that Aziz had been officially appointed pastor. He was still a full-time theological student at CNTC, but he put his heart into preaching and was the first of a succession of student pastors.

By then the rains had started, and with them came plagues of sand flies and mosquitoes. We practiced anointing with oil—oil of citronella, that is, passed from person to person during the night services. We also burned trash in buckets inside the shed, producing enough smoke to drive the pests away—and do bad things to our lungs.

Then one Sunday morning we arrived for service only to find ducks swimming on the floor of our shed. The area, part of the Caroni River plain, was low-lying and prone to flooding. Our neighbor Dan Dan, just across the street, invited us to hold services in his verandah and living room. We gratefully accepted and worshiped there for a while.

It took a long time for our floor to dry out. It was still muddy when we returned to the shed. All the benches fit on one end of the large platform, which sat high and dry on its concrete block foundation. So we held church that way awhile.

Before the year was out, Pastor Aziz and others began to sense that it would be better to have our own building. We investigated several possible locations, quite aware of the fact that our building fund was nonexistent. Eventually we decided to accept a small space in front of Goura's house.

A commercial firm gave us a truckload of heavy shipping crate material. These valuable crates had been used to ship cars from Japan to their local assembly plant.

Pastor Aziz spearheaded the mixing and pouring of a cement floor. It was set and curing by the first of December. Then the rains pounded for two days, delivering all the rain expected for the entire month. Low-lying streets and roads flooded. Fish were caught in the street and boats were used for taxis. Some suspected the gods were showing their displeasure over our little building project. Funny thing, though, our slab was never covered with water.

Pastor Aziz had carpenter friends in another church who, in a few days of hard work, put a half-

The Early Cratewood Chapel

wall building on top of our slab. Galvanized sheets were then nailed to roof beams. It didn't leak much —no more than strips of sealer could stop. On Wednesday, December 11, we had our first service in our still unfinished Early Cratewood Chapel. Eventually, chain-link fence above the half walls gave some security. Many more hours of work went into making it attractive and more suited for worship. Even our kind Hindu neighbors pitched in to mix and pour additional concrete for the driveway and front door entrance.

In the meantime, our little chapel had indeed become the house of the Lord. Hearty singing, anointed preaching, observance of the Lord's Supper, prayer for salvation, healing, and eventually one wedding and a funeral all witnessed to the inestimable value of this church house. At special times, the crowd was sometimes so large that the building couldn't hold it. Vacation Bible School spread out to several neighboring homes for classes. One night during a crusade, the street beside the church was literally filled with people. Best of all, some people started their walk with Christ in that Early Cratewood Chapel.

Bella, our pastor's wife, taught extra classes in the evening for school children. We celebrated Christmas with a program involving many children and youth and with an early morning Christmas service. And each year ended with a service, concluding with prayer around the altar (ahead of the start of firecrackers). Frequently we served refreshments after special services, giving an opportunity for hearty fellowship.

I think my favorite service of those early days was the Friday night prayer meeting. Instead of the traditional youth service, Pastor Aziz wisely decided to make it a service where everyone was invited, the main emphasis being prayer. There I frequently reminded the Lord that we were not in it for our health, but for His glory, and that He had to do something good.

Often we broke into smaller groups—children in one group, youth in another, adults in a third. We assigned a Christian adult to lead each group. One night I was assigned to the children. They were new to Christian prayer, so after asking for their requests, I lifted each concern to God audibly, asking the children to join in silently. Our group finished before the others, so we had a quiet talk.

Little Rajestrie spoke up. "But we're still Hindus, you know."

"Yes, I know," I answered softly.

Several years later, a more mature Rajestrie gave her heart to Christ. Today she is married to the superintendent of the Suriname District.

＊　＊　＊

In time I assumed the pastorate of the church. The community could not understand why student pastors did not continue for longer periods. Of course the reasons were varied and valid, some of them as simple as the fact that the pastor graduated from his program and needed to return to his home country. But since it seemed to be a problem, I finally agreed to be pastor, with the assistance of students. By faith we started a building fund and watched it grow.

Our congregation was also growing—not just in numbers but in people who had come to faith in

Christ. Thus on Sunday, September 1, 1991, we held a ceremony organizing the El Socorro Church of the Nazarene. District Superintendent Clifford Manswell officiated, and Rev. Dr. Joseph Murugan, president of CNTC, preached the sermon. Sixteen people were taken into membership, with 4 more joining the next Sunday, making a total charter membership of 20. Most of these were adults, and only two were transfers from other Nazarene churches.

Yes, that cheap little Early Cratewood Chapel proved to be a real house of God, set apart by His glory. We worshiped there until God gave us land of our own.

Three
GOURA AND HAMID

"Goura and Hamid, meet my Mom."

It was before our first crusade when Esther introduced me to these two individuals who would be firm allies in planting our church. Yes, even Hamid would be used by God even though he was not a Christian. Their little home was only two doors away from our borrowed shed.

Goura had been a secretary, but Hamid set his sights on her, wooing his prize until, by the help of others, she was persuaded to accept his proposal of marriage. He was from a Muslim background but actually followed no religion. A fisherman, he worked hard and owned his own boat.

At that time, Goura was a devout Hindu—so earnest that she became a leader in her community. She knew Hindi, the language of her forebears from India, and taught it to others. Her relatives had been worshipers of the fearful goddess Kali, but her father had refused to continue that tradition in his family. He would not make the required blood sacrifices. Some say he suffered the consequences in the near death of a son.

For Goura, life with Hamid settled into a pattern. She bore him five sons. He, in turn, became a typical jealous husband and a regular customer of the nearby bar. He worked hard, but with a little alcohol in him, he also fought hard. If he was late coming home, Goura would send one of the boys to peep into the bar and see if he was there. If so, she knew what she had to do. The boys were quickly fed supper and put to bed. Then she searched the house for every blade—anything that could cut—knives, scissors, the lot. These were all hidden so that at least she had a chance of surviving his drunken wrath. Many nights she had to run for her life. Her in-laws, close by, always gave her shelter and protection.

"Why, oh why, did I ever marry Hamid?" Goura wondered as she soaked her pillow with tears night after night. What a miserable existence! And she had no sense of God's comforting presence.

The boys were still small when the church on the other side of the highway started an afternoon Sunday School in Chanka Trace. Wanting to attend, Goura got the boys dressed and took them with her. But when she realized it was only for children, she started to return home. The boys began crying.

"Goura, you don't have to leave," the kind pastor told her. "Stay and listen."

So she sat down and did just that—Sunday after Sunday. The lessons were for children, but they were for her too. Her heart warmed at the thought of a God who loved her so much He was willing to give His only Son to die for her in order to forgive her sins. She reached out to Him, only to find that He was there, reaching out to her. What blessed relief and comfort.

When the church held crusades, everyone was invited back across the highway to worship with them in their building. Goura was the sole driver of the family car, and when Hamid was out to sea fishing on a Sunday, she went. But when he was home, he would not allow it. Thus many Sundays became depressing days knowing that her church was at worship, and she could not join them.

Getting her courage up, Goura asked Hamid for permission to be baptized. He refused. Time and again she repeated the request, only to be told no. Then one day when the church was having baptisms, Hamid was out to sea. So Goura presented herself for baptism. She carefully dried her hair before going home, and it was a long time before he learned about it—too late to do anything except fuss.

Eventually Hamid stopped his drinking. Things had come to a head one Christmas when he drank so much it made him deathly sick. The doctor treating him gave him medication that made him feel worse before he got better, and he warned Hamid that to drink again could kill him. Life became a little better, but it was far from easy.

It was at this time that Hamid, Goura, and I developed a genuine friendship. He made no objection to her attending our services, and soon she became a strong member of our group.

When Pastor Aziz and the rest of us sensed the need for our own place of worship, we talked it over with Hamid and Goura.

"There is room between our front wall and the street," Hamid generously offered. "That boat has to go out to sea anyhow."

"What about Tante Jessie?" I wondered. She was Goura's old aunt, solely dependent upon her niece. "She waves to her friends through that window, and we would be shutting off her view of the street."

"Never mind," Goura assured us. "She wants the church there so she can listen to the services."

The chain-link fence above the half walls still allowed Tante to watch the road and wave to her friends. And now she could attend every service without leaving her room. Her window looked out on the platform. Not surprisingly, she worshiped with us, made her choice for Jesus, and eventually requested baptism. We carefully walked her into the little sanctuary, sat her on a back seat (she had done well to come that far), and baptized her by sprinkling.

Even after Tante became bedfast, she still worshiped with us. Her dresser mirror was situated so that from her bed she could watch the platform.

Then she had a stroke. Before going to the hospital, she called the pastor and me into her room. Her speech was slurred, but she made it clear that she wanted her funeral service to be held in the church. A short time later, we granted her request with a full house of family and friends.

Most Sunday nights Hamid stood outside in the dark and watched all that went on. He could still smoke, but at least he was there. On more than one occasion he confessed, "I love it!" And he was quick to share anything he thought could help. He had almost a jealous care that we be thought well of. I appreciated his advice.

But not everyone appreciated Hamid. Some people refused to come because it was in his yard. My argument that it was the house of God, not Hamid's house, didn't persuade them. Some of these people promised to come when we moved (by no means did they all keep those promises). Nevertheless, we usually had good attendance for each service.

Throughout this time, Goura was not well. Over the years, several doctors diagnosed her with fibroid tumors. The last one said that if she had any

Goura teaching a children's Sunday School class

more problems, she would have to have them removed by surgery. The problems continued. At the close of a Wednesday night service she quietly shared this information with me. I wondered if her frail body could recover from major surgery. Calling together the Christian women present, we held hands in a circle and prayed. A few days later Goura shared the good news: the doctor had found no trace of fibroids, and her trouble ceased.

After some years, she and Hamid migrated to New York. In 2002 I was privileged to visit them in their lovely home. Both were working hard to support their American dream. By a wonderful turn of events, Hamid had been able to return to the sea for a living. Goura kept careful track of their finances, making sure their bills were paid on time. Colorful flowers bloomed in the front yard, and live greenery graced their living room—all the product of Hamid's horticultural skills.

We had a wonderful afternoon of lunch and fellowship with much to talk about.

Finally Hamid said, "Doc, I'm just the same as I always was."

"No, Hamid," I objected. "You're a lot nicer than you used to be." Spontaneously I came around where he sat, bent down, and planted a light kiss on his forehead. One day I believe He will invite Jesus into his heart. Many of us are praying for that miracle.

Four
DAN DAN

"Dan Dan is dead!" The unbelievable news reached me at the college. Quickly I drove to the church.

Sudesh—Dan Dan's son—rushed over and wrapped his teenage frame around me, sobbing. "Daddy was calling for you to pray with him."

"I didn't know. I'm so sorry," I said as I held him. Then together we hurried across the street to be with his mother, Mona, and the other children.

Most likely embarrassment had kept the family from making contact with me sooner. When Trinidad's most notorious drug lord needed to "disappear" for a while, Dan Dan and a friend took him by fishing boat to Venezuela. On the return trip, the boat hit a rock and the prow split open. Only by continuing at full throttle could they avoid filling with water and sinking. Suddenly the coast guard was upon them, ordering them to stop. Their continued run for the shore at high speed made it look like an attempt at escape.

Once on shore they were searched, but no incriminating evidence was found. I was told that in an effort to force a confession, they were beaten. Dan

Dan was not a well man, and now his condition demanded medical attention. Eventually he was moved to Port of Spain General Hospital where a policeman stood guard over his bed.

The family visited and prayed with him. Eventually he tried to escape and received further injury. His frail body could take no more; death claimed its victim.

I questioned Mona about the content of their prayers. "We prayed in Christian, not Hindu," she assured me. Dan Dan had heard the gospel numbers of times. Hopefully he turned to Jesus in repentance and faith.

I was not surprised when Mona asked me to say something at his funeral.

"I'll be glad to, if you will get permission from the pundit [Hindu leader]," I replied. She assured me she would.

Dan Dan was my friend. His house was directly across the street from the shed in which we first held services. When floodwaters turned our venue into a duck pond, it was his home that temporarily housed our services. He also helped mix and pour cement for the driveway to the Early Cratewood Chapel. And for years we used his veranda for adult Bible classes on Sunday mornings.

When Dan Dan and Mona legalized their relationship with a Hindu ceremony, I was one of the few invited guests. It was held upstairs in their drawing room. When it was time to sign the register, Dan Dan picked me as one of the two official witnesses. The pundit didn't know me; his curiosity was evident. Dan Dan didn't let that stop him, though. I was his friend. He could tell the pundit about me later. And so I signed.

When their daughter Lima married, and most of the village filled their yard, Dan Dan again chose me as an official witness. By this time the pundit had seen me at enough funerals that he didn't need to ask my identity. But Lima's new in-laws wanted to know who I was. Dan Dan proudly said, "You see them two Hindu priests we had there? Well, she more important than all ah them put together."

Most of Dan Dan's children came to our services. He and Mona came only now and again. But it was not unusual for Dan Dan to listen to the adult Bible class and, on rare occasions, request prayer. When I urged more regular attendance, he assured me that when we had land for a permanent church, he would be right there with me. There was something about meeting in his neighbor's yard that put him off. But he liked the church and seemed attracted to the gospel.

Dan Dan's front yard became the regular parking spot for my car. It was not unusual to be invited in for a refreshing drink or something to eat. The family made me feel at home.

Now Dan Dan was dead. He could not keep his promise of regular attendance when we moved. But I would keep my promise to Mona and prepare a little Christian message for his Hindu funeral. I prayed, and God gave me what to say. Days went by, with the family trying in vain to contest the autopsy verdict of "death from natural causes." Every day I prayed and prepared my heart.

While I do not know the hearts of those who attended Dan Dan's funeral, my prayer is that God will speak that message of hope again and again to them.

Finally the day of the funeral came. I arrived early and wept with the family. I took a seat up front so the pundit could see me. He conducted the ceremony and was about to step aside so the body could be taken to the river for cremation. I thought, "I guess I won't be speaking."

Just then Lima's father-in-law stepped up behind the pundit and whispered something in his ear.

"A request has come," the pundit announced, "for the reverend here to say a prayer. We'll ask her to come."

"Thank you, sir," I said as I rose and came to the head of the bier. I began by comparing Jesus weeping with His friends at the tomb of Lazarus to our sympathetic tears. "But Jesus wept with more than sympathy," I continued. "He wept because He knew death ought not to have been part of human experience. Death entered because of sin. And Jesus came to do something about that. The Bible says, 'For God so loved the world that he gave his one and only Son, that whoever believes in him shall not perish but have eternal life. For God did not send his Son into the world to condemn the world, but to save the world through him' (John 3:16-17)."

Briefly I laid out the claims of the gospel and sensed God's special anointing.

While I do not know the hearts of those who attended Dan Dan's funeral that day, my prayer is that God will speak that message of hope again and again to them so they may receive the offer of eternal life through Jesus Christ.

Five
RAMESH

A stroke had stopped Ramesh's wild living in Canada. He recovered enough to return to Trinidad, to his mother's home, but one leg was almost useless. A four-footed cane gave him limited mobility. He could not bathe or dress himself. His wife and grown son lived in a small apartment nearby, but as he put it, "The ember of love had been soaked in water too long to have any spark left." Even his brothers disdained him, so on his faithful mother fell the burden of caring for Ramesh.

We chatted briefly one Sunday afternoon when his cousin took me to visit Ramesh. He was Hindu, but I asked if he was interested in coming to church. He was, only there was no way to get there. "I'll come for you tonight," I promised, and told him when to be ready. I kept my word, to his surprise. Of course he was not ready. But the next week, he was dressed and ready to go. Later he said others had offered to take him to church; I was the only one who had actually come for him.

Ramesh listened to the service and made an immediate response to the gospel invitation. Certainly he did not understand everything, but he knew he needed help. So he kept on coming.

The congregation quickly embraced him. Now and then his faithful mother would also come. When she was busy sewing the beautiful wedding clothes with which she made a living, one of his Christian cousins helped bathe and dress him. Sometimes I had to wait or return for him, but it was rare for him to miss either of the Sunday services or the Wednesday night service. It became clear that his heart had changed. He became a beloved brother to his church family.

Ramesh's favorite hymn was "I'm So Glad Jesus Lifted Me." He often requested we sing it as the words said exactly what had happened in his life: Jesus had turned him from hopelessness to hope. He—and we—prayed for his healing, and a little feeling did return to his foot. "If God heals me, I'll get a car and pick up people and bring them to church," he declared. But eventually he concluded that God had given him *inner* healing. Even a Hindu pundit who knew him noted the difference. Ramesh told him why, and the pundit advised him to continue with "whatever" had helped him so much.

One year several people from our church attended a district adult retreat, including Ramesh's cousin Seeram and his good friend Paul. Seeram and Paul promised to take care of Ramesh, and his mother consented to his going. I drove them to the camp, but soon realized he'd have to climb stairs to go into and out of the cabin. Seeram and Paul took care of that by lovingly carrying him when necessary. The whole camp warmed to him. At the end, Ramesh came home with notes from many people expressing deep Christian love. These he proudly showed both to his mother and me. At church he testified, "I have been loved by many women, but never have I experienced such love as the people of God gave me."

Ramesh lay helpless as a baby, and it was impossible to tell whether he recognized me or not.

Then one night my phone rang. "This is Ramesh's mother. He had a stroke. He is in ward 44 at General Hospital."

"I'll come right away," I promised.

Ramesh lay helpless as a baby, and it was impossible to tell whether he recognized me or not. Still, I talked and prayed with him, hoping he might hear me.

Others were there also—one brother and a favorite aunt. The four of us walked out of the ward together. Almost immediately his brother said, "What kind of funeral do you think he wants?"

"Christian," I said without hesitation. "He has been baptized."

"Christian," echoed both his mother and his aunt.

"Don't you think he would want a Hindu funeral?" the brother suggested. It was more than a suggestion. It was his vote. But there were three of us who voted Christian. His mother and aunt had been close enough to him to know his mind. And so it was decided that I would conduct the funeral at his beloved church. About 24 hours later Ramesh went home to heaven, never having regained consciousness.

Other family and friends seemed to have some say in the situation, however. I was instructed to go to his home and lead in the singing of his favorite song, in keeping with Hindu tradition. Then his body would be taken to the church for the service.

"You'll want me to pray at the house, too, won't you?" I offered.

"No, just lead in his favorite song," came the emphatic reply.

I went to the home and met a large crowd of family and friends. Most of the church people had already assembled at the church, so the song I led was almost a solo.

When we were finished, I hurried to the church to meet the procession. I waited and waited. Apparently as soon as I left, a sadhu (Hindu holy man) stepped out and removed his shoes. Then he went through a Hindu ceremony. Only when it was complete did the hearse bring the body to the church.

We had a good service with God's smile on it. A large crowd sang God's praises and recalled what a blessing this brother had been. I preached the gospel and gave Ramesh's testimony—from despair to hope through Christ.

Before we left for the cremation site, a small delegation approached me. "May we do a little Hindu business as we light the fire? Otherwise we could be in trouble. Please?"

I believe God gave me an answer. "I cannot give you permission to do it. But neither will I stop you if you do." Of course they did it.

On the banks of the Caroni River, the Trinidad version of the Ganges, Hindu cremations were in progress both to the right and to the left of us. This was a government-selected site for open-air cremations. But our service was truly Christian, with Scripture reading, praying, and singing during the burning until we could sing no more.

Ramesh has not been forgotten. The fragrance of his changed life lingers still. And to this day, every time I hear *his* song, I smile.

Six
GOD'S SOMETHING BETTER

"I look at land for Chanka Trace every time I'm in Trinidad," Regional Director James Hudson exclaimed during one of his visits. It was true that I had shown him several possibilities.

We prayed for land. We looked at land and talked to owners and agents. We added to the building fund. Finally, I thought we had found the perfect place. "Lord, I believe You for this land or something better," I prayed. But the high price being asked for it was not reduced one penny.

There was another piece of land, more to the heart of the village. Several mentioned it to me. My casual glance at it did nothing to make me think it was right. Finally I agreed to see it as it was about the only vacant piece I hadn't checked out. From the outside it looked too small, and besides, I thought God had something better for us. But with a good peek over the vine-burdened fence, I saw it was larger than I had thought. It was also centrally located, the ground had been built up and leveled, and it was fenced completely around except for the very wide gateway.

My positive reply had no hint of uncertainty, in spite of the fact that our building fund was approximately $10,000 short.

The owner was away in India, but the real estate agent, Jit, said his price was $250,000 TT.* I talked this over with District Superintendent Manswell; we agreed that $200,000 would be satisfactory.

When the owner returned, Jit and I met with him and his wife. After some small talk, I asked, "So how much do you want for the property?"

"Make me an offer."

"What about $180,000?"

"Too low."

"Well, what would you say about $200,000?"

"Yes!" he fairly shouted. "My wife and I have agreed that if you offer us that, we will sell."

"Consider it sold."

My positive reply had no hint of uncertainty, in spite of the fact that our building fund was approximately $10,000 U.S. short. However, two families in the Dothan, Alabama, First Church of the Nazarene came through with $5,000 each. We made the required down payment and three months later, July

---

*Currently $1 U.S. = $6.25 TT

The temporary building on the church's new land

1994, the final dollar was paid. God's "something better" was ours.

Village people said I was lucky. They talked about how many others had tried to buy this land and how the owner had refused to sell it. But the church and I knew it wasn't luck; it was God. And God's timing was perfect. Had we negotiated sooner, we wouldn't have been ready either spiritually or financially. The other piece of property seemed to be God's attention diverter while we prepared.

A hastily constructed wooden building was ready for the first service on our land upon my return from a short furlough. Associate Pastor Winston Baldeosingh and some of the young people worked until the wee hours of a Sunday morning in August to make it happen.

We invited the entire district to a dedication service on Saturday, October 22. Holding hands in a large circle in the middle of the property, we sang "Holy Ground" and felt the Spirit's presence. "A Glorious Church" was our final hymn after a good message by the district superintendent.

Monday, December 5, 1994, marked the actual beginning of work on the permanent church. God gave us many helping hands through which He worked to make the miracle possible. Some of these were Americans who came at their own expense. Our architect, Skip Brothers, and his friend Cliff Patnode came down from Florida several times with expert advice and workmanship, as well as architectural drawings that cost us nothing. Work teams from Alabama, Mississippi, and Indiana also contributed time, labor, and finances.

Locally we owed a debt of gratitude to Victor Griffith and Eleazar Noray—builders par excellence. Church members and friends helped and prayed and gave. An Alabaster grant supplied a big boost. And God gave me patience and persistence through long hours of waiting on officials to approve or disapprove permits for electricity, water service, and other utilities.

Not the least significant was the gift from Ca-

The dedication of the new church building

ribbean Nazarene Theological College of the old tabernacle building. Its steel structure was still in good condition. Our church people cleaned and painted it, and soon it became the frame of the first unit of the new building—now the educational unit. We moved into it in June of 1995 with a grand opening service. A crowd estimated at 250 packed the place, filling the benches and rented chairs.

The government drainage ditch along the main road in front of our property was unpaved and very irregular. Water could stand a long time in some of its holes, creating perfect mosquito breeders. It also looked bad. We showed it to the government representative in charge of such works for our area. He promised help, and eventually a few villagers were paid for 10 days each to pave that ditch. "A 10 days on the road" was a sought-after boon.

We built a low, concrete block wall right across the front of the property, seated on the heavy foundation of the government stone wall. The tops of the concrete blocks needed filling and sealing off. The pile of stone fragments left lying on the side of the road was perfect filling material. While others were doing jobs requiring skilled labor, here was a job I could do. So with long sleeves and a broad-brimmed hat, I went to work. From down in the ditch I could reach the fragments on one side and deposit them in our wall on the other. People stared. Cars slowed down. One friend stopped his car and asked what in the world I was doing out there working in the hot sun. "I got a 10 days on the road," was my laughing reply.

In September we began the second phase of the building program—the construction of the permanent sanctuary. Together the two phases would create an L-shaped building. By the end of the year, we had a complete skeleton of the sanctuary—foundation, steel frame, and roof.

My time, strength, and the church's money were running out. I was due to leave Trinidad for my final furlough and felt clear that it was time for me to say farewell.

Inside the new sanctuary

At one point in the building process—before any work teams had come from the United States—we ran completely out of money and owed a small debt at the local hardware store. I told our treasurer that we could make no more purchases until the debt was paid. Troubled, she took it to the Lord in prayer. Later, both of us shed tears of joy as she shared the answer He gave through His Word: "Be strong and courageous, and do the work. Do not be afraid or discouraged, for the LORD God, my God, is with you. He will not fail you or forsake you until all the work for the service of the temple of the LORD is finished" (1 Chronicles 28:20).

God was surely faithful to His promise. I had not been in the United States a week when President Millard Reed of Trevecca Nazarene University told me of a sizeable monetary gift someone was prepared to give. He wondered if I knew a project where it could be used. Did I ever! The building was completed with the help of a Work and Witness team from Trevecca and the skill and building crew of our contractor. I flew down for the dedication on March 7, 1997, even though at that time much work remained to be done. I was invited back again to preach for a crusade in July in the newly completed sanctuary—truly a dream come true.

Seven
ALPHONSO

"Mr. Singh at the grocery store wants to speak with you," the message came to me for the third time.

While I was unusually busy with the building program and preparing for our first Work and Witness team, I decided it must be important. I walked down to the shop and was greeted by a smiling Mr. Singh.

"I have a sister whose one-year-old son has never been baptized," he told me. "The parents would like you to do it."

I had never met the parents, though I knew some of the family. Most of them were Hindu. "Maybe I wouldn't be able to baptize him," I began, "but I could dedicate him, provided the parents would agree to certain things. I would have to talk with the parents."

He agreed, and a meeting was soon arranged at Mr. Singh's home where I met little Alphonso (not his real name) and his mother. I explained to her that they would be promising to rear him as a Christian, taking him to church and so forth. She agreed to everything. About the time we were through, in sauntered Alphonso's father—a handsome, suave Indian with a strangely familiar face. I felt I had seen him before, but I couldn't imagine where or when. Briefly I explained the pledge to him, and he assured me that was fine.

"Now when do you want this done?" I asked.

"Just as quickly as possible."

"Well, what about next Sunday?"

"That would be fine."

"Do you want it in the morning service or the evening?"

"Oh, we would rather have it at home. It would be so much more convenient for us."

They were not from my church or even from that village. And I was sure they would want to have a little celebration at home with a full meal. So, rather reluctantly, I agreed to come the next Saturday and have the ceremony at their house.

Saturday came, and I picked Mrs. Singh up at the shop. She was my guide to Alphonso's home. When we were near a sizeable town, she directed me off the road and into a new subdivision. The houses were two-story concrete, well-built, and nicely set in large lots of land. Alphonso's home was no exception. The entire place was enclosed by a high concrete wall, and the driveway was beautifully paved. Straight at its end, built into the wall, were four dog kennels with matching wrought-iron gates, each barring the way to a ferocious-looking, large, black dog. I turned left into the ample carport by the kitchen door, right beside a new white Toyota.

In the kitchen, Alphonso's parents busily put the finishing touches on our dinner. Soon the father excused himself and went upstairs.

"Your husband looks so familiar," I ventured. "I think I've seen him somewhere before."

"You probably have. He's in San Juan a lot," she replied. But that told me almost nothing. San Juan was a very large area, and my church was in the extreme southern end. Going into the living-dining room area, I saw a man and a woman, neither of whom I had met. I introduced myself. They were the godparents. I sat beside the godmother and made some light conversation. Noticing her accent, I asked where she was from.

"I'm from Colombia," she replied.

At the time, I didn't think twice about it as I often meet people from all over the world in Trinidad. Only later did I understand its significance.

At last Alphonso's father returned, and everyone gathered around the dining room table for the ceremony. Never before had I dedicated a child sitting down, but they wanted it that way. The mother and both godparents answered a clear-cut "yes" to my questions, but the father looked at me, creased his handsome face with a half smile, and gave a curt little nod. I figured that would be the most I got out of him, so I finished the ceremony.

The two men went outside immediately, and the lady of the house began dishing up our meal. She handed me my plate, and I held it, waiting for the others. But the other ladies began eating as soon as they were served, even though we were still standing.

"Would you mind if we had the blessing over the food?" I interrupted. My hostess looked embarrassed.

"I forgot how to ask it," she stammered.

"Never mind. I'll ask it." So I did, and we sat down at the table to eat together.

The meal finished, Mrs. Singh and I said our farewells and left. On the way back to San Juan, I asked again about Alphonso's dad. "Your brother-in-law looks so familiar. I think I've seen him somewhere before."

"Oh, you probably have. He's in San Juan a lot," came the same answer.

"He's not a businessman or something?" I fished gently.

"Yeah, he owns a little store," she said hesitantly. But a little store didn't seem enough to account for the home I had seen for a fairly young couple with their first child.

I dropped off Mrs. Singh at home. Across the

junction, near her shop, stood one of my friends. Calling him over, I asked about Alphonso's dad.

"And he drives a brand-new, white Toyota car?"

"Yes."

"He's a drug lord, and don't go there again. It's not safe." He also knew the godmother from Colombia. She, too, was involved in the drug trade. Now it made sense.

I was stunned. I had prayed for God to bless me and make me a blessing in their home. Now I felt a sense of defeat. That feeling persisted until the next morning when I awoke to prepare for church. I stood in front of the kitchen sink rinsing out my breakfast dishes and talking to the Lord.

One Saturday night a few weeks later I decided to read the newspaper before bed. On the second or third page a caption caught my eye: "Supermarket Proprietor Shot Dead."

"Lord, I went to be . . ." and it was as if I heard or felt Him say with me, "the guest of him who is a publican and sinner." And quickly He seemed to add, "So did I." The defeat was gone.

I sent the dedication certificate to Alphonso's parents, along with a letter reminding them of the pledge they had agreed to and urging them to bring Alphonso to church. I told them they were welcome at my church, but that if they did not feel comfortable about that, they should find a church perhaps nearer to them where they could go.

One Saturday night a few weeks later I decided to read the newspaper before bed. I spread the *Guardian* out on the dining room table. On the second or third page a caption caught my eye: "Supermarket Proprietor Shot Dead." With horror I realized that the name was that of Alphonso's father. A look at my record book confirmed it. From the description of where it was, I realized I had come upon the crime scene the day before. On my way home from town, I encountered a line of parked cars just as the road widened out near the pass between two valleys. While there was a considerable amount of policemen, no one stopped me. So I eased on through wondering what it was all about. Now I knew. His body was found behind the wheel of his white Toyota car, a single bullet through his head.

On my way to church I stopped at Mr. Singh's grocery store to offer my condolences. On Tuesday I attended the Hindu funeral at the family's home. I told Alphonso's mom I was praying for her and would continue to pray. I have asked many others to join me in this.

Why did the Lord allow me to become involved in such a thing? I cannot believe it was chance. He had some purpose. Someone once suggested that

Alphonso might preach the gospel some day. At the very least I pray he will become a strong Christian man.

Eight
MAMA

She was an ordinary woman with an extraordinary amount of tragedy in her life. Ten years before we met, her mother was murdered early one morning on her way to sell in the market. Five years later, her youngest son suffered a fatal burn. Five years later still another son, on drugs, took his life. Then a few years later her brother committed suicide. Perhaps no one else I have ever known has had so much heartache in her life.

This precious woman sorely needed to know the peace that Jesus gives. She lived within reach of my church, so together with the pastor and his wife I went to her home where we presented the gospel. Both she and her husband came with us to church.

In spite of the fact that this woman was several years younger than me, I learned to call her "Mama," just as her seven surviving children did. Life had aged her terribly. She had borne nine children for her husband—eight sons and one daughter. Yet he never once told her he loved her. He worked hard but drank heavily, venting his frustrations on her at will. The strenuous gardening she did regularly in

Mama

the hot sun also took its toll, as did arthritis, diabetes, high blood pressure, cataracts, and glaucoma. Only the pain in her heart was greater than her physical pain.

"Papa," her husband, ceased his church attendance as abruptly as it had started. But eventually Mama and three of her children began to walk with the Lord. A daughter-in-law and three grandchildren also came. Eventually all eight were baptized and joined the church.

Mama loved feeding her family and me. Rarely did I stop by to take her to church without her begging me to come in and have something to eat. She was a good cook, and I enjoyed her spicy Indian fare. Sometimes after church she invited anyone in my car to come join us at her table. She became a real mother to many of us. And when we left for home, her parting admonition always was, "Drive careful. Get home safe."

But life continued to be difficult for Mama. Family conflicts took their toll, and there was no end to the hard work. In time, Mama became a more stable Christian and began to intercede for her family. She sometimes prayed the entire night on her bed. But attending church was a problem. The approximately one mile would have been nothing had it not been for a very busy highway. With failing eyesight, she took a risk every time she crossed it. I gave her rides as I could, but when I left for furlough they ceased.

In 1999 I was asked to return for a three-month stint as interim academic dean at CNTC. It was with great joy that I resumed my old post—and very soon visited Mama again. She rejoiced! "Pick me up for Sunday morning and night, and Wednesday night, Sister," she requested. Once again she could count on being in church regularly. Even if I did not come on Wednesday night, she was still there. For almost four full weeks she attended. Her son said he never saw her more happy than at that time. This in spite of the fact that things were not well at home, and her physical pains were growing progressively more difficult to bear. She confided in her sister that she would rather die and go on to a better place.

Commencement weekend at the college was soon upon us, and we had a nice banquet planned for one of the evenings. Paul, a senior student and now pastor at El Socorro, was to take Mama's daughter Rita as his escort. I was to drive them. Shortly before time to go, he was at my house explaining that he would be a bit late. That wasn't like him. He hinted at needing to tell me something, but he chose to get ready first. Finally, in the car, he broke the news. Mama had been hit on the highway and killed that afternoon. He was struggling with deep emotion; Mama was like a real mother to him.

Of course Rita would not be going to the banquet. But Paul was one of the graduating seniors, expected to make a speech. So we went with heavy hearts. I marveled at Paul's composure. His speech was well-done, with no hint of the tragedy he and his church had experienced.

After the banquet, we went straight to Mama's home where neighbors and family had gathered. Upstairs, where we could talk privately, Mama's son

Seeram told us that she would want me to preach her funeral. Arranging the time of the funeral proved to be difficult. Close family living next door had a wedding planned for Sunday. Finally it was settled to have the funeral Monday morning at ten o'clock. That was the day of graduation, but it couldn't be helped.

True to tradition, many gathered at the home around the casket on Monday morning. The service was simple consisting of a song; a reading from 1 Corinthians 15, the "resurrection chapter"; and prayer. God blessed His Word as we felt a real sense of His anointing in the reading.

Hurrying to the church, and hoping to be ahead of the crowd, I found that many had already arrived. The church was soon packed. Extra benches were brought in, but they quickly filled up. How thankful I was for our beautiful sanctuary—still too large for our regular services, but adequate for this crowd. Pastor Paul took charge, Mama's favorite soloist sang and led the singing, and I preached. My prayer was that God would be glorified and that her testimony might come through loud and clear—to Christians, Hindus, Muslims, family members, and whoever else. I believe He answered that prayer.

My text was John 11:37, "Could not he who opened the eyes of the blind man have kept this man from dying?" My message outline was a three-fold answer to that question:

(1) Yes, He could have prevented Lazarus's death temporarily had He chosen to, just as He could have prevented Mama's death.

(2) However, He could not revoke the death sentence pronounced by God on sinful man.

(3) Instead, He took the sting out of death, the victory out of the grave.

I sought to emphasize the victory Mama had through Christ.

In conclusion I said, "When I dropped Mama off one week ago Sunday night after church, as usual she said, 'Drive careful. Get home safe.' More than anything else in all the world, Mama would want her family to get home safely to heaven at the end of the journey.

"As for Mama herself, she has no more bad eyesight, no more arthritis pain, no more trouble with her sugar or her blood pressure, and no more scorn from those who saw her only as a poor, illiterate gardener, not recognizing that she was a daughter of the King. She is in God's presence, and she is whole and well and beautiful."

Seeram had strayed from Christ, but upon Mama's death he realized how much he needed the Savior. Alone he repented and returned. Today he is happily married to a strong Christian woman, and together they are serving the Lord.

Rita struggled terribly over her mother's death.

But today she is serving Christ alongside her pastor husband, Ralph Marshall.

Papa also suffered over his loss—the bride to whom he never professed love. Before I left for the United States, I reminded him, with tears, that Jesus loved him enough that He died for him. Pneumonia snuffed out his life in late 2002.

Now I pray for Mama's family every day. I remind God of the prayers she prayed and ask Him to honor them. Seeram also is an active intercessor, taking up where Mama left off. We are thankful to serve a God who hears and answers our petitions.

Nine
KESHORE

"May I call you Mom? I didn't love my own mother until I met you."

"Of course you may, Keshore," I replied with pleasure. Keshore was a teenager who had attended the Sunday School that preceded our own. Now he was in fairly regular attendance in our services. His older brothers were cocaine addicts, and it was reported that even his mother was selling it. But Keshore saw what it did to the other boys, and he chose never to use it.

Eventually, however, he did join the drug trade —as a pusher. His brother's life was at stake; he joined to keep him from being killed. But nothing I or Aruna, his girlfriend, could say availed to make him stop. For a while he went deeper and deeper, becoming extremely "successful." Then when he was thoroughly disgusted with himself, he gave notice of quitting. Unfortunately, the web in which he was entangled was never completely broken.

During the good times, Keshore seemed completely right with God and man. Then he would relapse and go back to pushing. He coveted "the good life," and without much education, pushing drugs was the only way he knew to ensure it. There is no telling how many times God in His mercy delivered him from death or a living hell on earth.

One night while I was out driving I saw Keshore walking alone along the road. I stopped.

"Hello, Keshore. How are you?"

"Things tough, Mom. Things tough," came his reply. It was evident his spirits were low and he was in no mood to talk.

"Well, Keshore, I love you," I said, then drove away.

Later Keshore said to me, "Remember that night you stopped and said you loved me? Well, I had a gun in my pocket and was on my way to kill a man who had stolen my cocaine. After you said you loved me, I couldn't do it."

Another time, while I was working at the college, Keshore came to my mind. I prayed for him. Later he told me a car full of thugs had come looking for him at the intersection by his home.

"Where's Keshore?" they demanded of the curb sitters.

Knowing these were bad guys, and that they were armed, his friends gestured unhesitatingly toward Keshore sitting on the opposite side of the street.

Keshore was hustled into the car at gunpoint.

Ruth with Keshore, Aruna, and their sons, Aaron and Brandon

But as they started to leave, the engine stalled and died. It was a stolen car; they had no key. The men jumped out, abandoning both the car and Keshore. This was right during the time God had brought him to my mind.

Eventually Keshore married Aruna in a simple ceremony I performed in my own living room. A comfortable handful of friends and relatives witnessed it. Later, Aruna's mom gave a small reception at her home.

Aruna loved the Lord, and Keshore tried to as

well. Theirs should have been a happy marriage; sometimes it was. But there were also difficult times when past entanglements hindered the growth of their relationship. Nevertheless, God blessed them with two bright and precious boys—Aaron and Brandon.

Keshore loved his parents and grieved deeply when his dad died of complications brought on by chicken pox. A few months later, his mother died of asthma as she was being transported to the hospital. Now I was the only "parent" he had. You would have thought our family extremely large: all his brothers and sisters and all the boys on the block had long ago learned from him to call me "Mom." But it was only Keshore whom I introduced to relatives and friends as "my son."

As I was finishing my last bit of packing before leaving for retirement, Keshore came to my home. Since he couldn't really help me, he sat outside on the verandah with Brother Lenny, a longtime employee of the college, and the two of them cried together. The next morning Keshore, Aruna, and the boys were at the airport to see me off.

Every time I returned to Trinidad, I looked forward to seeing them. If Keshore was distant, I knew he was into pushing. He stopped trying to hide it from me.

In late summer, 2001, I was preparing to teach in Guyana for a month when the phone rang. It was

Keshore. We chatted a while, and he said he and his family wanted to see me when I made a stopover in Trinidad. He said his son Aaron had graduated from kindergarten and was doing well in school. (Aruna told me later that Keshore had cried over his graduation. He was the first person in Keshore's family ever to graduate from anything.) I looked forward to seeing them all and hearing him teasingly call me "Old Lady."

My teaching assignment in Guyana was almost over. It was now Friday, August 31, and that morning I had read my Bible as usual and looked for a special verse to write in my spiritual life diary. Isaiah is full of special verses, but I finally settled on 65:24: "Before they call I will answer; while they are still speaking I will hear."

Shortly after lunch the phone rang. The secondhand message was simply, "A man in Trinidad named Keshore died this morning. Do you know him?"

"Yes," I said. "He was my son." I began to cry.

Had I prayed for Keshore that morning? I could not remember doing it, though I prayed for him daily. Then quickly the scripture in Isaiah came: "Before they call, I will answer." It seemed to be

God's assurance He had been with Keshore when he died and that he was in heaven.

My efforts to contact Aruna by phone were in vain. But the next week, when I was in Georgetown, her sister called. I told her about my experience with the scripture verse and the sense that he had gone to heaven. "We all feel that way," she replied. Then Aruna came on the phone and filled me in on details.

Keshore had been kidnapped on Wednesday. A ransom was demanded and paid. On Friday morning the kidnappers called to tell where he could be found. His friends took him to the hospital, damaged beyond repair. He had multiple injuries: broken legs, spine, and ribs; liver and heart damage; and punctured lungs. Aruna was beside him. He told her he would die.

"No, darling. We've been through tough things before, and together we'll make it through this."

"No, I'm going to die."

She knew he had been praying, doubtless a heartfelt prayer of repentance. Now in intense agony, he gathered the strength to pray one last time, "Jesus, help me! Take me!" And just that quickly he was gone.

Keshore's Hindu brothers and sisters wanted a Hindu funeral. Aruna insisted it would be Christian, in the church, and after that they could do whatever they wished. So after a service blessed by God, they held a Hindu ceremony and cremation.

As I meditated on this young life so brutally ended, the marvel of God's grace has come to me afresh and anew. While Keshore didn't deserve to go to heaven, I know that neither do I. It is only by God's grace given freely through His Son that any of us can make it. I have been made to weep and rejoice at the wonder of that grace. Words fail me to tell the Savior how thankful I am for His atoning death—for Keshore, for me, for all of us. And I stand amazed at the realization that God's Spirit was there, drawing Keshore, enabling him to repent and believe.

Ten
PAUL

"Who is she, and what does she want?"

These and other suspecting thoughts obviously swirled through the minds of Paul and his siblings as they stood looking at me. The four teenagers, whose Sunday afternoon video I had interrupted, looked surly and resentful and very much on guard. I was as apprehensive as they were. How was I to "straighten out" their teenage minds and behavior at the request of their mother? Especially teens I'd never seen before, and in a situation I didn't fully understand? "Oh Lord, help me," I silently, fervently prayed.

Their mother had come to church one Sunday night in response to a friend's invitation. From her backseat she stared at me on the platform. "What kind of a church is this, and who is that?" she seemed to be asking. After church I went directly to her.

Her name was Virginia Bunsee, and she was of Lebanese parentage. Her father had come from Beirut as a young man, and her Lebanese mother had migrated to Trinidad from Martinique. Virginia's parents eventually became Port of Spain business people, owning a store. Their lives revolved around that store. Plagued with emotional problems, Virginia found little help or sympathy from them. When she fell in love with an Indian man and married against her father's wishes, the breach became an immense gulf.

The emotional problems of her youth followed her, and her husband eventually decided he could take no more. Winding up his Trinidad affairs, and declaring himself at the United States embassy as single, he obtained a visa and left for New York. He promised to send for the family in due time, but soon the money stopped coming and all communication ceased.

Shortly after our first meeting, Virginia came to the church. "I want my husband and I want him *now!*" she demanded loudly and emotionally. Obviously she was in great distress and seemed to expect some miracle from me. I explained that I had no power to help her. She stormed a while longer until the pent-up emotion had been discharged. It was a pattern she repeated often.

Then came the Sunday she invited me home for lunch and to meet the children. What she really wanted was for me to tell them to shape up. In response to my desperate prayers, God enabled me to speak gently and carefully. "Children, your father's absence is hard on your mother. Please try to help her all you can." Quickly, but not soon enough for them, they retreated to the bedroom to continue their video, and I heaved an inward sigh of relief.

The children were still young. Paul was apprenticed to his father's friend to learn how to be a goldsmith and silversmith—one last kindness done by his father. And right away his new skills had to be used in support of the family. By nature a very responsible boy, he felt great pressure. As he put it, "I had to become a father before I was ready." He completed high school, but Kelley, one year older, quit school and went to work in a restaurant.

To let Virginia stay had been an unintended violation of the rules of my mission. Sadly, it fell my lot to return her to the hospital.

The girls' school careers came to a screeching halt, by decree of their father, when the family moved to Chanka Trace. Paula, still underage, went to work at a movie theater, married, had a son named Christopher, and separated—all before she was out of her teens. Liz stayed home, was eventually readmitted to school, and earned her high school diploma. But the loss of time and momentum had taken its toll. She became much more skilled in human relationships than in academics.

Virginia was a good cook and loved her children, but her frequent hysterical episodes made life diffi-

Paul Bunsee

cult for the family. Eventually the four teens shuffled her off to the hospital. After a short stay, she was released and found her way to my home. I agreed to let her stay two days while she located another place to live. She stayed two and a half months.

I found her no easier to get along with than did her children. "Oh Lord," I prayed, "if somehow you can be glorified by this, then it's OK." But it was difficult, and I could not see how God was being glorified. To let Virginia stay had been an unintended violation of the rules of my mission. Sadly, it fell my lot to return her to the hospital.

Paul knew I had sincerely tried to help. He seemed to feel more sympathy for his mom too. Eventually he persuaded the others to let her come home.

Paul had begun to attend our little church. Several factors influenced him. A friend had committed suicide, Liz had started attending and brought home a friend from Paul's primary school days, and I kept on inviting him.

During his first visit, he was impressed with the friendliness of the people. We sang "I Know the Lord Will Make a Way for Me," and Paul certainly wanted a way made for him. But what did it mean to live a holy life? Eventually at an altar of prayer he invited Christ to come into his heart, and he began to find out.

Seeram, Mama's son, was a fairly new Christian at the time as well. The two young men became like David and Jonathan. Every Sunday night after church they went to the highway walkover bridge and had a prayer time together. They encouraged each other at every opportunity.

One Sunday night, however, they realized something was missing. They talked it over and prayed about it but still felt spiritually dry. Paul came to me with the problem. I advised a total commitment to Christ, asking that His Holy Spirit sanctify through and through. A short while later at a public altar, Paul made that commitment and received the Spirit's full-

Paul as pastor of El Socorro

ness. He told me, "I don't want to just be a Christian;
I want to be all out for God."

Sensing that God might be calling these two men
to preach, I suggested the church give them a local
preacher's license. Seeram agreed but Paul didn't. He
later confessed, "My head was saying 'no' and my
heart was saying 'yes.'" By the next year he sensed the
call so strongly he accepted the license.

Paul became president of the local youth group.
Actually, he became a pastor to them. He also took
an active role in public worship services, leading the
singing, and doing whatever else needed to be done.
I wanted him to go to CNTC and receive training to

be a pastor, but I wondered how it could ever happen, given his home responsibilities.

When a Work and Witness team came from Alabama, my sister Becky and her husband, Jerry, were among the members. They were quite impressed with Paul. Before they left, they offered regular scholarship assistance to enable him to go to CNTC. His boss allowed him to continue working on a part-time basis, and the college education he needed became a reality.

In his final year of school, the El Socorro pulpit became vacant, and Paul was asked to pastor his home church. In spite of his extra off-campus responsibilities, he kept up his grades and continued to be a fine Christian example to other students. Consequently, he was elected by the student body to receive the Good Citizenship Award for seniors. He continued to pastor El Socorro for five years, becoming widely known and loved in the community. In 2004 he earned a master's degree in Christian counseling. Today Paul serves as an associate pastor at St. James Church of the Nazarene, part-time lecturer at Caribbean Nazarene College (formerly CNTC), and school social worker with the Trinidad and Tobago Ministry of Education. He was also ordained in April 2006.

"Ministry is challenging and exceedingly rewarding," Paul said recently. "I love the Lord and I love people. I have so much to be thankful for."

Eleven
GOD ISN'T FINISHED YET

"When will you turn El Socorro over to another pastor?" I was asked more than once.

"When I find someone who loves it as much as I do," was my ready reply.

For five years Paul Bunsee was that someone. Then God selected another.

Farouk Mohammed was born into a traditional Muslim family, his wife, Vilma, into a Catholic home in Brazil. Vilma gave her heart to Christ during a crusade service. After she married and moved to Trinidad, her spiritual hunger led her to the San Fernando Church of the Nazarene.

Farouk had despaired of finding satisfaction in his traditional worship. He remembers, "Whenever I visited the place of worship, there were among the worshipers the 'elite.' All they did was discuss business: who had how many stores, cars, money, etc. This turned me off." So he began going to another venue, only to find the same thing. For two years he absented himself from public worship but continued to observe all the other religious practices. He describes that period: "There was an emptiness in my life that needed filling. I was happily married to a committed wife, had one child, a good job, and my own house and car. The comforts a young man longed for, I had them all. But that still was not what can fill this void." Unbeknown to him, Vilma and others were faithfully praying that he would let God fill the void.

One day after work, Farouk was waiting to get a taxi to go home. He heard a voice say, "What you want, I have it." He turned to look, but no one was there. He concluded his conscience was playing tricks. But it happened on another day. And then a third time.

"What is it you have that I want?" he responded.

And very distinctly he heard, "You want, when you die, to be in My heaven."

It was true, so he asked immediately, "What do I do?"

"Accept my Son, Jesus Christ, as your Savior."

Without further question he did so. He joined Vilma in church attendance and at the earliest opportunity made public his decision for Christ. Soon after, he and Vilma were both baptized.

The Mohammeds became exemplary Christians, studying the Bible and participating wholeheartedly in church. Then God called Farouk to preach. He began taking courses in preparation, still

Pastor Farouk Mohammed at the gate to the church grounds

holding onto his supervisory position with the Ministry of Works and Transport (by now he and Vilma had three children to provide for). He preached as opportunities came.

When asked to consider taking the El Socorro pastorate, Farouk and Vilma prayed until God gave clear guidance to accept. Since May of 2002 they have been faithfully serving as pastors. Their Sundays, as well as many other days, are spent in the village fulfilling the duties of their calling. And both of them have become students at the college to better equip themselves for ministry.

The church's influence is being felt in the community. Several members of the Chanka Trace Village Committee (forerunner of a village council) are members of the church or have a strong connection to it. For want of a community center, regular meetings are held in the church's educational unit.

On a recent trip to Trinidad, I worshiped at El Socorro. I witnessed a beautiful scene: an entire family together in church with the parents coming forward for prayer. It was the husband's public declaration of his newly made decision to follow Christ. After the evening service was dismissed, we stood around for a while, enjoying the presence of Christ and each other. The new Christian turned to me and declared, "I've decided to change my life. Thank you for building a church here."

✳   ✳   ✳

The Church of the Nazarene came to Chanka Trace not to fight Hinduism, Islam, nor any other religion. We came to lift up Jesus as the One who died for all—the only Savior from sin.

The love in my heart is an outflowing of God's love. It has been a two-way street; I have enjoyed being loved by Chanka Trace in return. But my prayer is that it will not stop with me. May it reach to the very heart of God. May many more of these, my beloved, come to full faith in the One who loves them more than I possibly can, the One who gave His life on the Cross that we might live unto God. I covet for Chanka Trace a great turning to the Savior. Only then will life be what it ought to be: family loving family, neighbor loving neighbor, former enemies becoming brothers and sisters, sharing the very life of God within.

Satan fights at every step trying to defeat that vision. But God is greater and has won victory by Christ's death and endless life. Let's pray and believe Him to make it happen.

Chanka Trace, I still love you! And God isn't finished yet.

CALL TO ACTION

In response to the information in this book, please consider praying for the following requests:

1. The Church of the Nazarene in Chanka Trace and the unique challenges it faces. Pray especially for a continued outpouring of God's Spirit to draw the people of that area to Him and for His protection on their lives.

2. The individuals mentioned in this book, that God would care for them, guide them, and use them to reach out to others who don't know Christ.

3. The president, staff, and students of Caribbean Nazarene College.

4. Ruth Saxon in her retirement years, that God would bless her for her service to Him.

—Aimee Curtis, editor

PRONUNCIATION GUIDE

The following information will assist in pronouncing some unfamiliar words in this book. The suggested pronunciations, though not always precise, are close approximations of the way the words are pronounced.

Aziz Abidh	ah-ZEES ah-BID
Bella Abidh	BEL-lah ah-BID
Baldeosingh	bahl-DAY-oh-sing
Caroni	CA-roh-nee
Chanka Trace	CHAHNG-kah TRACE
DiVali	di-VAH-lee
El Socorro	EL soh-KOH-roh
Eleazor Nora	yel-ee-AY-zohr NOH-ray
Farouk Mohammed	fah-REWK moh-HAHM-ed
Ganges	GAYNG-jees
Goura	GOH-rah
Guyana	guy-AN-ah
Hamid	HA-mid
Jit	JIT
Kali	KAH-lee
Keshore	ke-SHOHR
Lima	LEE-mah
Moya	MOY-ah
Murugan	MUR-uh-gan
Mungroo	MUHN-grew
Rajestrie	RA-jes-tree

Ramesh	RA-mesh
Sadhu	SAH-dew
Seeram	SEE-rahm
Singh	SING
Tante	TAHN-ti